*Do It Right
the First Time!*

OTHER BOOKS BY
JACLYNN WEBER

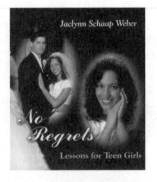

*No Regrets—
Lessons for Teen Girls*

LESSONS FOR TEEN GIRLS

Do It Right the First Time!

by Jaclynn Weber

Copyright © 2006

CHRISTIAN WOMANHOOD

8400 Burr Street • Crown Point, Indiana 46307
(219) 365-3202

ISBN: 0-9745195-6-1

All Scriptures used in this book are
from the King James Bible.

CREDITS
COVER DESIGN: Linda Stubblefield
PROOFREADING: Rena Fish

Printed in the United States of America

Table of Contents

Foreword by Todd Weber 7

Chapter 1
Thanksgiving Day—Every Day! 11

Chapter 2
How Will You Fill Your Page? 17

Chapter 3
Do It Right the First Time 23

Chapter 4
Daddy's Girl 31

Chapter 5
Not My Will 37

Chapter 6
    That's Not Fair! 43

Chapter 7
    Half-Empty or Half-Full? 47

Chapter 8
    Something Little That Makes a Big
        Difference 51

Chapter 9
    A Good Name 59

Chapter 10
    Dating With a Good Name 65

Chapter 11
    Rising Above Your Name 71

Foreword

by Todd Weber

$\mathcal{J}$aclynn Schaap and I started dating in September of 1999 as freshmen in college. Our first date was the Chicago Boat Ride sponsored by Hyles-Anderson College. We recently celebrated our fourth wedding anniversary. As a testimony to Jaclynn's heart and soul, which are her qualifications to write this book, I want to share our story.

As a sophomore in high school, I remember seeing Jaclynn at a Youth Conference in Louisville, Kentucky. My first thought was, "Wow, she's beautiful." At that time, however, I thought that she was a senior in high school; therefore, I dismissed all possibilities of meeting her or getting to know her. Then, during my senior year in high school, Hammond Baptist High School was coming to play in the soccer tournament that my team, State Line Christian School, was hosting. One of my friends told me that Jaclynn Schaap was a cheerleader, and he and I argued about the fact that she was not a cheerleader because she had graduated two years before that. He was insistent; I thought I was right...but he won the argument two days later when she showed up in Temperance, Michigan!

I think I said a total of nine words to her during that tournament—I was always a big talker. But I had a second chance that year when our school went to the Hammond Baptist basketball tournament. I again saw Jaclynn and said three words to her! I basically didn't talk to her or see her again for about seven months until I went to college in September of 1999.

In college, I knew she was the one I wanted to date. I was told by some to date around, but I knew I did not have to date around; when you start dating perfection, you know you do not have to date around to find someone better! Obviously, I was not good enough in those early days because she still dated around, but that's another story!

I told Jaclynn that I loved her in the spring of 2001. By the fall of that same year, we were engaged, and we were married on June 1, 2002, and we've been honeymooning ever since!

On our first date in 1999, Jaclynn and I sat on a bus on our way back to the college from Chicago; we talked about many things, but one of the topics of our conversation was the fact that we had saved ourselves for each other. I had kept myself clean and pure for my future wife, who ended up being Jaclynn, and she had kept herself clean and pure for her future husband, who ended up being me. Jaclynn did right throughout her dating years—just as she did right in so many other areas.

In the seven years that I have spent getting to know my wife, I can honestly say that my life has been increasingly richer, fuller, sweeter, and more fun.

At the writing of this book, Jaclynn and I have a 15-month-old daughter Lyndsay, and Jaclynn is due with our second child in two months. God has been very good to us.

I believe that Jaclynn has been given a special gift of communication. More importantly, I see Jaclynn every morning reading her Bible and praying by our rocking chair in the living room. Because of that, she has something worth communicating. The title of this book is the story of her life. She has done right the first time in every area of her life.

CHAPTER ONE

Thanksgiving Day— Every Day!

I love everything about the holidays, and I'm always a little sad when they are over. Yet, the reason for the holidays should never be forgotten but remembered the whole year through. Just like on Thanksgiving Day, we are supposed to be thankful and kind to our family and friends; we are supposed to live that way every day of the year.

My generation is a very spoiled generation: everything we could want has been handed down to us. Not only do we live in America, but we have the very latest in fashion and technology and everything else. If you are poor, that probably means you do not have a cell phone, and most of the poorest kids in the slums of Chicago or New York City have cable television and the Internet.

We have no idea what suffering is really like, so we cannot even begin to imagine going without food for a day or walking to school barefoot because our parents could not afford a car or a pair of shoes. I'm not saying we all need to walk barefoot to school (in five feet of snow, uphill both ways if your grandparents are telling the story!), but we do need to learn to be grateful for what we have been given.

One of my friends was recently sharing with me about her Sunday school class. She teaches junior high girls who all attend a Christian school. She had a theme for the fall program, and every week she would bring the girls something that went along with her theme. One week she wrote them all a note, and along with the note, she gave them a small gift. Immediately, the girls read their notes, looked at each other's notes, and said, "They all say the same thing!"

Then one girl held up her gift and asked, "What is this for?" as if to say, "Why did you give me this worthless piece of junk!" My teacher-friend felt so badly about her notes and gifts.

I am not trying to say you should jump up and down and hug each person who gives you a piece of candy, but the selfishness and greediness need to go. What happened to the gratitude we had on Thanksgiving Day? Is it gone, not to be found, until next Thanksgiving?

There is a young man who greets our church people coming in every service. This man is one of the friendliest and one of the happiest people you will ever meet, but he is handicapped. He knows my name, and he smiles big and says "hello" every time I walk in the doors of our church.

Last night as I was coming in, he gave me a

cinnamon gummy bear to eat. I took it and thanked him, then put it in my purse and walked away. Should I have torn open the wrapper and shoved it into my mouth and shaken his hand over and over while thanking him profusely? That might have seemed a little strange! Should I have thrown it on the floor and started smashing it with my foot while yelling, "I hate cinnamon bears! Don't you know that by now? Why can't you give me something that I like?"

While neither of these responses would be appropriate, the first one would definitely have made him feel better than the last. Or is it not important how other people feel—as long as I get what I want?

Girls, how you make that Sunday school teacher feel about what she does for you is so much more important than what you get from her. How you make that grandma feel when she gives you the same green and yellow scarf she's given you for the past eight years is much more important than the fact that you have thrown them all away or shipped them off to the Salvation Army.

One of the greatest things my parents tried to teach me is that people are more important than things. Did you get that? **People are more important than things!** Your teacher is more important than the donuts she brings to class each week; your grandparents are more important than the digital camera they got you for Christmas; your youth director and pastor are more important than the activities and days off they give you.

You see, the ones you love will not always be here, but you can get a scarf anywhere. The people whom you take for granted now will one day be lying in a casket, and at that moment, the gifts and things don't matter. Are you going to look at the person's cold, dead face and wish you had been a little more grateful for that person?

Don't wait until it is too late; rather, make every day a "Thanksgiving Day" because people are more important than things.

CHAPTER TWO

How Will You Fill Your Page?

Everyone started out in life the same. We were like a blank page with no marks, cuts, or holes. We had not made any mistakes, we had our whole life ahead of us, and we had nothing to regret or for which we should be ashamed. There were no great deeds we had done, nothing great we had yet accomplished; we had so much potential. We had not been hurt by anyone; no one had taken advantage of us; no one had sworn at us or thrown their fist in our face. We did not know whether we were rich or poor, whether we had loving parents, or whether we were illegitimate. We did not know if the people who brought us home from the hospital were our biological parents, our stepparents, or our adoptive parents. We were new with no marks or indentations, and we had our whole lives ahead of us.

In just a few short years, however, some of our pages began to be written on with indelible ink that would last forever. Some of you came to realize that not all people are honest and good, and in fact, they sometimes act very selfish and evil. Your blank pages began to be marked up by those who you thought loved you. Maybe a father took advantage of you or a mother beat you when she got drunk, or you were sent to foster homes at a young age. Very early in life the pages in your book began to be cut apart and shredded with every evil device imaginable, and often you wished that you had known a better way or a better life.

Others of you, like myself, grew up in godly Christian homes where your page was patterned with love, prayers, and laughter. Parents who loved you taught you right from wrong and tried to shield you from evil and hurt. Your page stayed clean and unmarked by sin, that is, until you began to mark it up. You see, the love from godly parents and leaders was not enough for you. You wanted to do things your way and see what sin was like. You did things *your* way, and slowly you began making marks on your page. Maybe you tried drugs or alcohol or messing around with the opposite gender, and for a while, it was fun. But then came the car accident or the call from the doctor's office that you were expecting a child who would never know his father, and you realized your page was torn and ripped beyond repair.

Maybe you are in the first group of people and have seen a lot of hate and bitterness in your short life. As just a teenager, many of you have been rejected and feel that your entire life is worthless.

You do not know what true love is, and you are desperately searching for answers to your pain. You do not feel that God loves you, and you hate yourself. You do not understand why you were placed on this earth. Maybe you are even thinking that it would be best to end it all because you no longer feel that life is worth living in your situation.

Those of you in group two may think that you are enjoying life, but deep inside, a gnawing emptiness exists that tears away at your soul like a knife. You would never admit it to anyone, but you do not have the answers. Every party you attend only leaves you with more loneliness and regrets than you previously had, and each time you let down your standards and your morals, you despise yourself even more. You too are looking for the answer, and though you know where it is, you do not want to find it.

God gives each of us an empty page to fill, and it is called our life. He has a special plan for us, yet He lets us choose how we will fill it. Some of you are filling it with good, and others are filling it with evil. It is our choice because God does not force us to serve Him. He allows things to come into our lives for a reason, and whatever happens to us will work together for good if we will let it.

No matter how marred or torn your page has become, God has a plan for your life as long as you are alive. It may not be the perfect plan God once dreamed for you, but there is something special He wants you to do. My Grandpa Hyles used to say, "As long as a person is alive and breathing air, God can use him." God uses sinners, and I am so glad He does because that is exactly what I am.

To those of you who have not marred your page but have kept it clean and whole, please do not destroy it with sin and bitterness. God has so much He wants you to do, and you have your whole life ahead of you.

The greatest gift you could give to God and to those who have invested in you is your life. Don't ruin it with sin and rebellion, for it is not just your life you are ruining; you will also ruin the lives of your husband and your children and those who are coming behind you someday.

"Oh, may all who come behind us find us faithful;
May the fire of our devotion light their way.
May the footprints that we leave lead them to believe,
And the lives we live inspire them to obey;
Oh, may all who come behind us find us faithful."

Keep your page clean so that those who come behind you will see the love of God and the joy of serving Him instead of hurt, pain, and bitterness from a life that is beyond repair.

CHAPTER THREE

Do It Right the First Time

Have you ever done something wrong and you thought you got away with it, only to find out later that someone saw you and turned you in, or that your parents knew about it all along? There have been many times in my life when I have done wrong, but there have not been many times that I did not get caught and punished for what I had done.

When I was in third grade, I missed a couple of

days of school. When I got back, the teacher gave me a make-up sheet to take home for my parents to sign. I took it home, but it never made it out of my book bag, and the next day when it was time to turn it in, it was not signed. "I'll just sign my parents' names on the bottom," I thought to myself. "No one will be able to tell the difference!"

Obviously, I did not realize that my sloppy attempt at cursive writing was definitely different from either of my parents' distinguished signatures. I turned in the paper and thought nothing more about it.

Lunch time came and went, and sometime during the afternoon the principal called me to his office over the intercom. I quickly got out of my seat and headed down the hallway, wondering if I was going to be rewarded for something. What an unpleasant surprise awaited me in his office as I soon found out that I was not being rewarded at all. Instead, I was being punished for lying on my make-up sheet. Needless to say, I never signed my parents' names on my make-up sheet again!

I was a cheerleader for two years in high school, and we were going to our last basketball tournament during my senior year. It would be the last time I would ever cheer, and we were both excited and a little sad that this would be our last trip together. We went to Louisville, Kentucky, and we cheered and played all day. At the end of the first day, we stayed in a hotel where some of our friends from Arkansas, who were also cheerleaders, were staying. They asked us if they could come over to our room for a while, and we said that would be fine. However, our coach taped our rooms every night, and if the tape on the door was broken or gone the next day, everyone in that room was sent home. Well, we thought the girls could just take the tape off when they came in, stay for a while, and put the tape back on when they left. It seemed logical enough at the time, so that is what we did. I won't go into detail about everything that happened, but to make a long story short, it turned out to be the worst trip we ever took, and we all had a personal invitation to see the principal when we got back.

I told you these stories to show you that I am living proof that the verse in the Bible is true that says: *"...be sure your sin will find you out."* It seems that every time I did something wrong, the punishment I received was far worse than the enjoyment of the sin. Sure, I could tell you many other stories (too bad we don't have time or room!!), but the point is that my sin always found me out. My mom told us one time that every day while we were growing up she would pray that if my brother or I did something wrong, we would get caught. Now, I did not really appreciate her prayers then, yet many times, when I was tempted to do something wrong, those words would come to my mind, and I would do right simply because I knew God answered my mom's prayers and I knew I would get caught!

Let me ask you this question today: what are you doing that you think no one knows about but you? What sin are you committing that you know if your parents found out about, they would be heartbroken? What are you doing with your boyfriend that you know would get you kicked out of your Christian school if your principal found out about it, or worse, could ruin your life if you were caught?

Maybe you do not believe now that the Bible is true when it says: *"...be sure your sin will find you out,"* but you will be very sure it is true the day you get caught, and you will find out the punishment and the disappointment on the faces of those you love is ten thousand times more painful than the thrill you experienced for a while.

A sweet girl in our church who is happily married now and has an adorable baby wrote me a letter recently. In the letter, she wrote that she did not do things the right way when she started out, but how much she wants to do right now and wishes she had started her life out a different way. She wants so much for God to use her, and I know

He will, but she has some regrets. Does God love her, and has He forgiven her? Yes, He loves her and has forgiven her as much as He loves and forgives me. Yet, the same God Who is loving and merciful is also a jealous God and called "a consuming fire" in the Bible. He loves and forgives, yes, but He does not let sin go unpunished, and He is not a respecter of persons.

If you have a past you regret and are living it over and over in your mind day after day, you need to let it go. Start fresh today and look to the future. But if you are holding on to someone or something that you know you need to let go, then let it go NOW. There is no greater feeling than to have peace and a guilt-free conscience in your heart.

Don't wait until you have already ruined your life to turn it around. My grandpa, Dr. Jack Hyles, used to say, "As long as a person is breathing air, God has a plan for his life." He is the God of the second chance, but I don't want God to have to keep changing His plan for me. I don't want to get to the end of my life, only to look back and see the great things I could have had and then realize that I missed it all. I want this song to be the theme of my life:

> "Only one life, so soon it will pass;
> Only what's done for Christ will last.
> Only one chance to do His will,
> So give to Jesus all your days;
> It's the only life that pays.
> When you recall, you have but one life."

CHAPTER FOUR

Daddy's Girl

When my husband and I found out we were having a girl, we were both very excited. Girls are so cute and fun, and there are so many adorable little girl clothes which make them very fun to dress!

I know my daughter will love me, and I will love her, but I really want her to be a "daddy's girl." Her dad is already very excited about seeing her for the first time, and I think she'll have him wrapped around her finger before she's old enough to even say, "Dad"!

I love my mom very much, and we are extremely close today, but growing up I was always a
daddy's girl. I thought my dad was the strongest,
most handsome man in the world, and in my eyes
he could do no wrong. I went with him everywhere. We had a date once a week, and when I
was eight years old we started a bus route together
that now runs about 300 every week. My mom was
never jealous of our relationship and always
encouraged me to be close to my dad.

My dad was also a good listener. He would listen for hours (it probably seemed like days to him!)
to me about all of my ideas and stories and non-
sense, and then he would tell me how smart and
logical I was. I really don't think any child (espe-
cially a seven-year-old girl) is all that logical and
wise, but my dad always made me feel special. He
would pay me $1.00 for every ten minutes I would
rub his back, and then he would tell me how much
better he felt after I rubbed it, and that without my
backrubs he probably would be sick and have to go

to the doctor all the time. At the time, I soaked it all in, and I really thought that if Dad did not get a backrub from me, then he would get sick!

One of the wisest things my dad did for me, though, was when I became a teenager and started becoming a woman. For many dads, this awkward stage scares them, and they seem to pull away from their daughter when she actually needs him the most. But my dad, being a very wise man, pulled me closer to him at this stage of my life. He realized I needed him more than ever, and he made me feel even more loved and special.

When I was in junior high, my dad and I started going on our "weekly dates." When I was a 15-year-old girl, my dad would let me come sit on his lap and cry when I had a rough day. He still listened to me. He listened to me talk about my high school boyfriends and my crushes, even though I'm sure he got tired of hearing about them, and I still thought he was the strongest, most handsome man in the world.

As I got older and fell in love, I began noticing my dad seemed a little more distant and quiet. He didn't ask for backrubs every night, and he didn't push our date nights like he once did. I wondered what was different or what I had done wrong.

Then one day I realized that as I was getting older, my dad was growing older, too. I realized that just as I needed him to pull me to him as an adolescent, it was also my job to stay close to him. He needed to feel loved and wanted. I realized it was just as much my job to be close to my dad as it was his, and I needed to let him know I loved him and wanted to be with him.

Sometimes when dads seem like they are pulling away from you or are uncomfortable around you, it is because they do not feel you want or need them anymore. They seem so tough and strong on the outside, yet on the inside is a very tender heart that wants you to be his "little girl" forever.

The wisest thing you can do for yourself, your dad, and your husband someday is to get close to your dad now. If you have never had a good relationship with him, the best time to develop one is now. The saying, "How you treat your dad now is how you will treat your husband someday" is not only wise, but it is also true.

You can be close to your dad, and if you could see inside that strong, hardworking body, you would see a heart that is aching to be close to you.

Even though I am married, I am still a "daddy's girl." We still go on dates, and he still listens to me, and he makes me feel special. I am thankful for a husband who encourages me to be close to my dad because he knows that very soon he, too, will have a daddy's girl!

CHAPTER FIVE

Not My Will

*I*n March 2005, Todd and I welcomed a new baby girl to our home. I could hardly wait for her to arrive! I looked forward to seeing her face, watching her eyes open, and holding her for the very first time!

Of course, my dream was for her to be healthy and not have any problems. God fulfilled my dream and gave me a happy, healthy Lyndsay. I am sure every mother wants to have a healthy, normal baby—just like our Lyndsay. However, sometimes our dreams and God's dreams are very different.

I give piano lessons to three children who are in our special education department at school, and they are so fun to teach. David and Kimberly Brock (and another baby who did not survive) were triplets born to Reed and Bonnie Brock. Kimberly is one of the sweetest girls one could ever meet, but she is blind. She plays the piano by hearing the sounds and memorizing the feel of the notes with her fingers. She is quite a good pianist, and she learns very quickly. David has a disease which takes him to the hospital very often, and he has had many, many surgeries in his short life; yet, he never complains about not being able to do what other kids can do. David is a very happy-go-lucky kid.

I am sure Mr. and Mrs. Brock's dream was never to lose a child and have a daughter who is blind and a son who is very sick. They probably dreamed of what their children would look like and the bright future ahead of each of them.

I also teach a teenage boy named Nicholas

Comstock, who is confined to a wheelchair and who may be in that wheelchair for the rest of his life. I hope and pray that one day he will walk, but only God knows whether or not he will. Nicholas has a muscular disease that has caused his hands to curl, and he goes through therapy every week. His piano lesson is one of his favorite times of the week, and it makes my whole week just to see him smile and learn how to play a song. He is a very hard worker and a very happy person.

The Comstocks would probably never have wished that their son would be in a wheelchair, but I also don't believe they would trade him for any healthy boy in the world because they love him, and he is their son. The life he lives may not be what they had once dreamed for him, but they are doing the best with what they have.

God's ideas of what we need are not always what we think we need. It was not my idea to lose a baby through miscarriage; it was probably not Brother and Mrs. Bob Gray, Jr.'s idea to have a son who is not healthy; it was not our country's idea to have some Muslim terrorists crash planes into the Twin Towers in New York City a few years ago; yet, for some reason, God must have thought those things were good for us because He did allow them to happen.

What is going on in your life that is totally different than what you had dreamed would happen? Is your mom dying of cancer, and you don't know how much longer she will be with you? Is your older brother breaking your parents' hearts as well as yours, and you feel like he does not even care? Is your senior year, which is supposed to be the best, turning out to be the worst year you have ever had?

Maybe your life seems so different right now than how you pictured it would be, and maybe you would not have chosen the state in which you live, the church you attend, the parents you have, the friends with whom you go to school, or the color of your hair. Guess what? That is all a part of God's plan for your life; and whether or not it is your will, it is God's will because He allowed it to happen.

Does that mean that God is mean and uncaring or that He is trying to torture you and make life miserable for you? Of course not! God is an extremely loving God Who created you and wants the best for you. Maybe He is trying to test your faith and to see if you really believe He is real. Maybe He is trying to prepare you for something great He has for you in the future. I do not know why God does the things He does sometimes, but I do know that it is all a part of His will. The song says, "His eye is on the sparrow, and I know He watches me!"

We cannot control what comes into our lives, but we can control how we react to those things. Let me give you a few ideas that might help you face those things that do not seem fair:

- Thank God for everything—the good and the bad.

- Accept whatever God brings your way.

- Look up every verse in the Bible on "trust" and write down what you think it means.

- Look for the good things God does for you each day and write them down.

- Tell God exactly how you feel and ask Him to help you through whatever you have to face.

These ideas may seem silly or foolish to you, but I challenge you to try them. Even Jesus had to go through something that was not His will, for when He was being crucified on the cross, He looked up at His Father in Heaven and said, "*…not my will, but thine be done.*"

CHAPTER SIX

That's Not Fair!

A little girl is having fun and enjoying her grade school days—playing jump rope at recess, riding bikes, and learning how to multiply. Life is so easy and perfect, until one days she finds out she has a tumor and needs to have surgery. Life suddenly seems unfair.

An elderly couple has been married for over 50 years. They have enjoyed the good times and made it through the hard times because they have always had each other. Now, planning to enjoy their retirement days together vacationing in Florida and relaxing in Hawaii, she suddenly becomes ill. The doctors say she may not have long to live. Life suddenly seems unfair.

A teenage girl going through junior high and high school is loving life, dating, going to banquets, cheerleading, and making lots of friends. One day she goes to the doctor, and he tells her she has leukemia and will need to go through chemotherapy. Suddenly life seems unfair.

You know, life is unfair at times to everyone— even you. Many of you have already gone through tremendous heartache, and you have cried lots of tears. Some of you (like myself when I was a teenager) have not experienced any great trials or pain, and maybe you have not cried very much and have a hard time understanding those who do.

No matter what you have or have not gone through, you need to realize that hurt and pain come to everyone, and you do not really have a choice of what it is or when it comes. You cannot choose not to make the cheerleading squad instead of having a mother die of cancer, or to have a friend betray you instead of having your parents get a divorce. That is pretty much left up to God, and there is nothing you can really do about it except to pray.

There is one choice you can make, though, and no one else can make this choice for you. The only choice you can and eventually will have to make is how you are going to react when bad things happen. Are you going to get angry at God and become bitter because He did not give you what you thought you deserved? Are you going to go through life blaming other people, or are you going to learn to accept it as a part of life, maybe not a fun and exciting part but a part you will look back on as a time when you grew closer to God and a time when you learned to trust and depend on Him? I like to remember a song when I go through something that seems too tough for me to handle, and part of the song goes like this:

"Our Father knows what's best for us.

His ways are not our own.
So when your pathway grows dim
And you just can't see Him,
Remember you're never alone...."

If you decide to make the choice to accept and move on, you will find true joy; and you will also realize that yes, life is unfair, but, yes, you can make it.

CHAPTER SEVEN

Half-Empty or Half-Full?

$\mathcal{I}$ am sure you have heard people say, "Is your glass half-empty or half-full?" meaning do you look at life with a positive attitude or a negative one? Everyone has good things and bad things happen to him, and one cannot control the circumstances God brings into his life. The only thing we can control is our attitude, yet some people never even learn to control that!

My dad often says during his sermons, "I am not surprised when bad things happen to good people. I am surprised when good things happen to anyone!" He also tells the story of a pastor who was captured and sent to a prison camp where he was tortured and treated like an animal. He was there for months and months, barely existing on little food and nothing to keep him warm except for one small blanket. Sometime during the middle of the night, he heard a soldier cursing and complaining because he had to stand watch outside in the snowy, cold weather. At first the pastor ignored him, and then he started to think, "If that man were Jesus, would you give him your blanket?" He immediately replied out loud, "NO!"

But the words grew louder: "If this man were Jesus, would you give him your blanket?"

Finally, he got up, walked to the door of his cell, and stuck his bony hand through the bars to hand the soldier his blanket. "Here, Sir. You can have my blanket."

The soldier ignored his prisoner at first, but the cold and fatigue were too much to stand, so he walked to the window and snatched the blanket out of the pastor's hand, swearing as he retreated from the prison bars.

I often wonder if the soldier who took his blanket that night ever accepted Jesus as his Saviour because of that good man's testimony of faith, joy, and forgiveness.

I know the problems teenagers face can sometimes seem as horrible as this man's torture chamber, and just like him, you may see no end in sight. However, I think if this pastor could have a positive attitude through his miserable circumstances and even in his death, then it is possible for us to be positive through our own personal heartaches. Let me ask you a few questions, and I want you to answer them yourself.

- Are you so upset about your problems that you have forgotten someone else might need your help?

- Are you so depressed that you feel like life is not worth living anymore?

- Are you blaming yourself instead of trusting in God?

- Are you blaming God for the bad He has allowed to happen instead of thanking Him for the good things He has done for you in the past?

- Are you rebelling because you do not know how else to handle your problems and fears?

Let me remind you that the Bible says, "*...the joy of the Lord is your strength.*" It also says, "*A merry heart doeth good like a medicine....*" Mrs. Sharon Lewis, one of my high school teachers at Hammond Baptist High School, used to have a sign on her door that read, "When you look at the sunshine, you cannot see the shadows." Are you enjoying the sunshine, or are you depressed because it rained one day this week? Are you focusing on the bad or enjoying the good? It is your choice, and I am going to choose the half-full life—not the half-empty one!

CHAPTER EIGHT

Something Little That Makes a Big Difference

$\mathcal{I}$n the previous chapter, I addressed the subject of choosing to look at the positive instead of the negative things that happen to us. However, sometimes it is easy to become negative about everything that happens to us—good or bad! Teenagers are known (although it is not true all of the time) for being critical, cynical people. To be sure, I know some teenagers who are more positive and encouraging than many adults I have met, but many times they are few and far between.

Have you ever talked to a cranky older person who seemed to hate life? We used to sell candy every year in grade school, and I would always hate it when I asked an older person to buy a delicious candy bar for only $1.00 and they would snarl, "I can't eat candy because I am a diabetic," or "You are the ninth person today who has begged me to buy a candy bar! No way!" Well, it was fine if the person did not want a candy bar, but did the person have to be so rude about it? All I wanted to do was sell the candy bars, and how did I know that everyone else had chosen the same day to ask the person to buy candy?

Do you think that people all of a sudden become a grouch on their sixtieth birthday?! I don't think so because I have met some very happy elderly people well into their eighties and even their nineties who are some of the sweetest, kindest people I know. For instance, a lady in our church named Mrs. Harrington, who was my Mom's and

my Sunday school teacher when we were seniors in high school, is one of the sweetest people you would ever meet! My piano teacher's mother just passed away, and she was in her nineties. If you ever could have been around her, you would have found out that she had more energy than many teenagers I know. She was an extremely active lady who enjoyed life to its fullest.

I hate to say it, but many of you are on your way to having a "grouchy old person life" because of your cynical attitude. Everyone is weird and strange except, of course, you! And you are God's gift to mankind. In your eyes, authority does not know anything, your teachers are poor people who have nothing better to do with their life than to teach you, your parents are old folks who are too strict and don't know anything (even though they have lived at least twice as long as you have), and your youth director plans boring activities that you do not care to go to anyway. Your boyfriend is not going to the activity either because he is the one who convinced you that it would be dull and boring. The fact is, if you were not dating him, you might actually have fun on an activity.

Then there is your preacher. If you ever actually listen to what he says, it is only because he tells a funny story. You happened to be awake for five minutes during that service because you were passing notes down the row to your friend who also was completely oblivious to what the preacher was saying.

Does This Description Sound Like You?

You know, the truth is, if you got rid of your backslidden friends and stopped dating your boyfriend, then you might actually stop criticizing and instead enjoy your life! You say, "Mrs. Weber, you are being so cynical to me!" Well, have you ever thought for one second how your teacher feels every time she walks down the hall and hears you laughing about how weird she is or how you cannot believe she gave you ten demerits? Did it ever dawn on you that she might actually care for you and want the best for you? Your authorities might be saving you from ruining your life someday!

Another common attitude among Christian teenagers today is the judgmental attitude. You know, it's the look you give to that new girl who walks into your school the first day. Without even asking her who she is, you just assume by looking at her that she is a snob who is trying to steal your boyfriend, who hates you, and who is going to try to ruin your life. Maybe you should start giving people a chance instead of tearing them down so you will look better. If you have any kind of relationship with God at all, you will realize that security comes from God and you are no better and no worse than she is.

I know it may not be "cool" or "in" to be a positive person, but God does not think it is very "in" when you criticize or tear down someone whom

He loves and whom He created "in His image." Usually when someone brings a gun to school and shoots his teacher, it is not because he is the basketball star or the cheerleading captain. Usually, he is a misfit who is trying to teach a lesson to everyone who has "rejected" him. He feels unloved and unimportant, and he is trying to prove to the world that he is someone.

For a moment, try to look ahead of today into your future. Someday, hopefully, you will get married, and you will probably have a child who will eventually become a teenager. Do you want kids at school to treat your son or daughter the way you treat people now? That may seem like an eternity away, and perhaps you don't care right now how your kids will be treated. Just remember the law of sowing and reaping and what the Bible says about how you treat others. In Matthew 7:12a the Bible says, "*...whatsoever ye would that men should do to you, do ye even so to them.*" What do the ten commandments say? The Bible says in Luke 10:27,

"*...Thou shalt love the Lord thy God with all thy heart...and thy neighbour as thyself.*" As I have already mentioned, people are more important than things, and God happens to love everyone—not just the rich, the famous, the "normal," or the well-known. In fact, many times in the Bible God chose the "weird" people—the ones who did not quite seem to fit in—to do great things for Him.

If you feel rejected today, let me encourage you that God loves you exactly like you are, and He has something great in store for your life. If you are the one pushing everyone else down so you will look better, then just remember that God says your kind is the lowest of them all. It is time for you to get right with God and start treating people how you would like to be treated. The Bible does say that we are "*fearfully and wonderfully made*"—and that means everyone!

CHAPTER NINE

A Good Name

*W*hat is in a name? Some people were named after family members who were loved very much; others were named because their name means "strong," "courageous," or "angelic"; still others were named after great men and women in the Bible whose names are still famous today.

When we hear someone's name, we often think of something about that person. For instance, when I hear the name President George W. Bush, I think of a great leader and a courageous man who loves God and our country. When I hear the name Dr. Jack Hyles, I think of a loving man who gave up many things so that he could help reach America for Christ.

When I hear the names Britney Spears and Jessica Simpson, I think of girls who will do anything to make money and have their names on the cover of a magazine. When I hear the name Michael Jackson, I think of a person (man or woman—I do not know) who has a sick mind and obviously needs serious help.

Now I want you to put your name in the blank: When I hear the name ____, I think of ____. What do people think of when they hear your name? What will people think about you 50 years from now when they hear your name?

The Bible says in Proverbs 22:1, "*A good name is rather to be chosen than great riches, and loving favour rather than silver and gold.*" I don't think Hollywood knows about that verse—at least it does not seem like it by the way they live their lives. Money is their God, and they will do whatever they have to in order to get it. Ecclesiastes 7:1 says, *"A good name is better than precious ointment; and the day of death than the day of one's birth."* When you were born, you were given a name, and what you do with that name is going to be how you are remembered when you die.

Let me share a story. Two brothers were born into the same family. One brother worked hard every day and helped his father with his business as soon as he was old enough. He loved his father and wanted to please him in every way possible. He desperately wanted his dad to be proud of him, and he tried very hard to uphold the family name by the way in which he lived.

The other brother did not care very much about what anyone thought, and he was not concerned about the feelings of others, including his father. He endured his life at home until he was old enough to leave, and as soon as he had the chance, he took off and ran away from home. He lived a fairly wild life, partying and spending lots of money. People in town knew his reputation, and thus he succeeded in ruining his father's name.

However, when you waste your money, you soon run out, and at that time there was no such thing as a credit card. Very quickly he realized that his partying life was coming to an end. He was at the end of his rope, to the point that he was homeless. Well, guess where he went? Of course, he went home to the father whose name he had ruined.

If you have not yet guessed about whom I am talking, it is the story of the prodigal son from the Bible. The father had unconditional love for his son, and he accepted him back and threw a party for him. However, I am sure he was disappointed in the son whom he had trained and who took all that he could from him.

We have a name as Christians; we are called the children of God. We have a name to uphold, and that is the name of Jesus Christ. The way we live our lives determines the way people think about that name. Christians are some of the nicest, kindest, and most sincere people I know. There are also people who claim to be Christians who live more worldly, sinful lives than many unsaved people, and they are giving God a bad name.

Mahatma Gandhi once said about this group of people: "I would be a Christian if it were not for Christians." Does God love us no matter what we do? Yes! His love is unconditional, and we can never wander so far from Him that His love cannot reach us; yet His heart is heavy, and He is disappointed when we sin against Him and try to ruin His powerful name.

So, how you live your life determines what kind of name you will have. If you live to honor the Lord and your parents, your name and your family's name will be remembered with joy and happiness. If you choose to ignore the things you have been taught, you may think you are the only one who is affected, but, oh, how wrong you are! You destroy your parents' name, your family's name, your church's name, and the name of your Saviour Who gave His life so you could escape the flames of Hell.

"A good name is rather to be chosen than great riches." (Proverbs 22:1a) What kind of name do you have? Are you living to honor your parents or to destroy everything they have taught you? You can never change the name you have been given, but you can determine what people think of that name. I want to have a good name. How about you?

CHAPTER TEN

Dating With a Good Name

$\mathscr{I}$ was talking to a teenage girl who was very interested in a certain guy. Imagine that! The really interesting thing is that she is a really good girl, and the guy is not really a good guy. Even more interesting was the fact that he is not drop-dead gorgeous or even really popular, but she was very attracted to him. Now why would she be attracted to him? He is not rich or even well known, but he likes her, and that makes the difference. This is a pattern I see with so many teenage girls—even good teenage girls—who fall for someone (many times a poor Christian) simply because he likes her. Girls tend to think that if they do not get a lot of dates, something is wrong with them. Dating is pushed so much (way too much) often starting in grade school, and by middle school, girls are dating seriously or steady. It sounds harmless and silly, but obviously it is not.

I know, as a married woman, it is easier for me to say, "Just be patient and wait. The right one will come along."

You think, "Yeah, right. She doesn't know what I am going through."

I did not always feel this way. My high school years were not a serious dating time, except for one person whom I dated steadily for a couple of years. We broke up during my senior year, and I really wanted to meet the person I was supposed to marry right then and there. I was the most impatient girl in the entire world I am sure, and my faith that God had someone just for me was wavering. The only problem with dating my husband at that time (who I did not even know existed yet) would have been that I had four long years of college after high school, and I knew I would never last dating the same person for that long. I was not one of those "slow-and-steady-wins-the-race" type of people! That day I wanted to know my future, and whom I was going to marry right then, and where I would be in ten years!

God did lead my husband and me together, but it was in His timing, not mine. Todd had to date and write other girls for a while first, then ignore me almost my entire first year of college before God and he thought it was time for us to start dating. God definitely was trying to teach me patience, and He still is by the way!

I can say that it is definitely better to wait and marry the right one than it is to hurry up and marry the first thing in pants that comes along. Some people with whom I went to school got married right out of high school because they just couldn't wait, and they were divorced not too long after they said their vows at the altar. Girls, when you say those vows, it means you are committing yourself to someone forever or until he dies (without your killing him)! Commitment is not something to be afraid of, but it is something to be taken seriously.

The country and western star who sang, "Stand by Your Man" had many husbands in her lifetime, and that did not bring her a good name. Divorce and split marriages do not bring a better name. Rather, divorce hurts your name and the names of your children and of everyone involved.

You should also never date anyone who is below your level spiritually. I am not saying that you are better or worse than anyone else. I know everyone is equal in God's eyes, but that does not mean you should date everyone. If the guy you are dating is into pornography, **you** are not going to change him. If he is being inappropriate with other girls while he is dating you, **you** are not going to change him.

There was a guy who was interested in a certain girl, and she acted like she liked him. She flirted with him and tried to be around him as much as she could. Several weeks later the young man learned that she was being inappropriate with another guy. Is that young man going to help her by dating her?

The Bible says in Proverbs 6:26, *"For by means of a whorish woman a man is brought to a piece of bread: and the adulteress will hunt for the precious life."* He will be brought down to her level if he decides to date her.

- Don't date someone who lies to his parents.

- Don't date someone who hates his father or mother.

- Don't date someone who criticizes authority, even if he thinks he is funny.

All of these are signs of someone who does not have a good name and someone who will bring

your name down and one day leave you with a ruined reputation.

I want to leave you with one thought that I hope you will remember your entire life: "It takes a lifetime to build a good name but only moments to ruin it." My junior high Bible teacher, Brother Chris Tefft, used to quote this statement by Dr. Bob Jones, Sr., quite often: "Never sacrifice the eternal on the altar of the immediate." Don't get impatient for the right one to come along, girls. Remember, your reputation is more important than the filling of a guy's lustful appetite. You are better than any of that, and don't you dare think for a second that you are not worthy of God's best.

CHAPTER ELEVEN

Rising Above Your Name

My Grandpa Hyles' father was the town drunk. Practically every night he could afford to, he went to the bar and drank away his sorrows until he could not remember anything. Often my grandpa would have to go looking for him early in the morning and try to get him to come home. He did not seem to care much for my grandpa and his family. All he cared about was drinking. My grandpa grew up with everyone knowing him as the son of the town drunk. What a name to try to live up to!

My grandpa would probably have grown up in his father's footsteps had it not been for his mother, Coystal Hyles, who taught him from a very young age that drinking was wrong, that God is real, and that church and the Bible are important. She saw what drinking had done to her and her family, and she did not want the same thing to happen to her son. She decided to help her son, Jackie-boy Hyles, to rise above the name of the "town drunk's son."

If you knew my grandfather, then you know that he did rise above that name, and he became one of the greatest preachers in the world. I am sure it was not easy for him to overcome his father's name, and his father was not much help in encouraging his son to do better than he had done. Yet, he somehow decided to do something more with his life than getting drunk every night.

I do not know what kind of family you come from or what kind of background you have. I do not know if you are white, black, Hispanic, Indian, or Filipino, and the truth is, it does not really matter. Every one of you girls, with God's help, can rise above the life that has been set before you. You just have to want it badly enough.

I have received letters from teens whose mothers are prostitutes; whose parents are divorced and remarried, and they struggle with their stepparent; who have tried to end their lives because of their circumstances; and whose mothers or fathers are dying of a terrible disease.

A girl with whom I went to school goes to our church, and I see her often. I asked my dad about her the other day because I always see her in a wheelchair, and one of her daughters pushes her around. He told me her story, and I wanted to sit down and weep for her when I heard it.

She has an illness that is killing her, and she cannot walk, so she has to be wheeled everywhere she goes. Last year she could talk, but her talking was slurred. Now she cannot speak, so she uses sign language to communicate with people. She has three children under the age of eight who have to help her do everything. She is married to a man from another country. In 2001 he went home to visit some family members; while he was there, the terrorists bombed our country. As a result, he could not get back into the United States. For the past five years, she has been trying to convince the government that she is dying and wants to see her husband again, but so far it has been in vain. Still, the officials will not allow him back into the country. Of course, she cannot work to earn enough money to fly him back here. Her life is filled with pain and agony, and I wish I could do something to help her. This woman, through her trials, continues to faithfully attend church with her children, and she is teaching them how to make it through anything life brings their way.

I know some of you may have parents who are on drugs or who hardly ever come home, and when they do, they pay no attention to you. Some of your parents may be going through a depression in their life and are acting like children as they make foolish decisions that affect your life. You can overcome any name you have been given, any circumstance you are facing, and any injustice that has been done to you. However, you can only rise above these problems with God's help.

Sometimes though, it seems like the worst kids in the school have the best parents. The parents who have done everything to give their son or daughter a good name stand by helplessly as they watch their precious child reject everything he has been taught and ruin their testimony and name. The Bible says, "...*Honour thy father and thy mother: that thy days may be long upon the land....*" This verse says that I am supposed to honor my parents—no matter what kind of name they have given me. I am supposed to honor them and do my best to uphold or better their name.

What are you going to do to honor your parents and bring them a good name? If your youth director knew what music you were listening to, would he think differently of you? If your boyfriend's parents knew how you and he were acting, would they be shocked and devastated? Are you helping your friends to have a better name, or could you not care less what people think about them? Are you just using them to get what you want?

You have within your power the ability to make a good name for yourself and others and to live a life honoring to those who have invested in you. You also have the power to take a good name and ruin it beyond repair—hurting the lives of everyone you know. Are you the reason your dad had to resign his church? Are you the reason a family left your Christian school to attend a public school so their teenager would not be around you?

What kind of name are you going to leave your children? If it is not important to you now, one day it will mean everything in the world to you, and you will either say, "I wish I had," or "I'm glad I did…."